Heroic Dogs

SEARCH AND RESCUE DOGS

by Dale Jones

Consultant: Denise Sanders
Director of Communication, Search Dog Foundation

BEARPORT
PUBLISHING

Minneapolis, Minnesota

Photo credits: Cover and 1, ©Daryl Pederson/Getty Images; 2, ©Matt Benoit/Shutterstock; 3, ©Erik Lam/Shutterstock; 4, Courtesy Library of Congress; 5, ©Noska Photo/Shutterstock; 6, ©Belish/Shutterstock; 7, ©Nazarii Karkhut/Alamy; 8, ©NSC Photography/Shutterstock; 9, ©jasomtomo/Shutterstock; 10, ©Artyom Geodakyan/Getty Images; 11, © Tap10/Shutterstock; 12, ©Malivan_Iuliia/Shutterstock; 13, ©Stoyan Yotov/Shutterstock; 14, ©Urban search and rescue/Alamy; 15, ©Richard Nixon/Alamy; 16, ©Nick Veber/Shutterstock; 17, ©Urban search and rescue/Alamy; 18, ©petographer/Alamy; 19, ©Tierfotoagentur/Alamy; 20, ©blickwinkel/Alamy; 21, ©skynesher/Getty Images; 22, ©AAron Ontiveroz/MediaNews Group/The Denver Post via Getty Images/Getty Images; 23, ©Eric Isselee/Shutterstock

President: Jen Jenson
Director of Product Development: Spencer Brinker
Senior Editor: Allison Juda
Associate Editor: Charly Haley
Designer: Colin O'Dea

Library of Congress Cataloging-in-Publication Data

Names: Jones, Dale, 1990- author.
Title: Search and rescue dogs / by Dale Jones, Denise Sanders, Director of Communication, Search Dog Foundation.
Description: Minneapolis, Minnesota : Bearport Publishing Company, [2022] | Series: Heroic dogs | Includes bibliographical references and index.
Identifiers: LCCN 2021007346 (print) | LCCN 2021007347 (ebook) | ISBN 9781636911182 (library binding) | ISBN 9781636911274 (paperback) | ISBN 9781636911366 (ebook)
Subjects: LCSH: Search dogs--Juvenile literature. | Rescue dogs--Juvenile literature.
Classification: LCC SF428.73 .J66 2022 (print) | LCC SF428.73 (ebook) | DDC 636.7/0886--dc23
LC record available at https://lccn.loc.gov/2021007346
LC ebook record available at https://lccn.loc.gov/2021007347

For more information, write to Bearport Publishing, 5357 Penn Avenue South, Minneapolis, MN 55419. Printed in the United States of America.

Contents

Rescue in the Rubble

The shaking may have stopped, but the **earthquake** has done its damage. And a little girl is lost in the **rubble**!

Luckily, the best search team is on the scene. A four-legged rescue worker climbs over a fallen wall, sniffing as it goes. Suddenly, the search and **rescue** dog smells something and starts barking. People rush to dig out the girl. She is saved!

Dogs have been helping find people for a long time. Search and rescue dogs were first used in the 1600s.

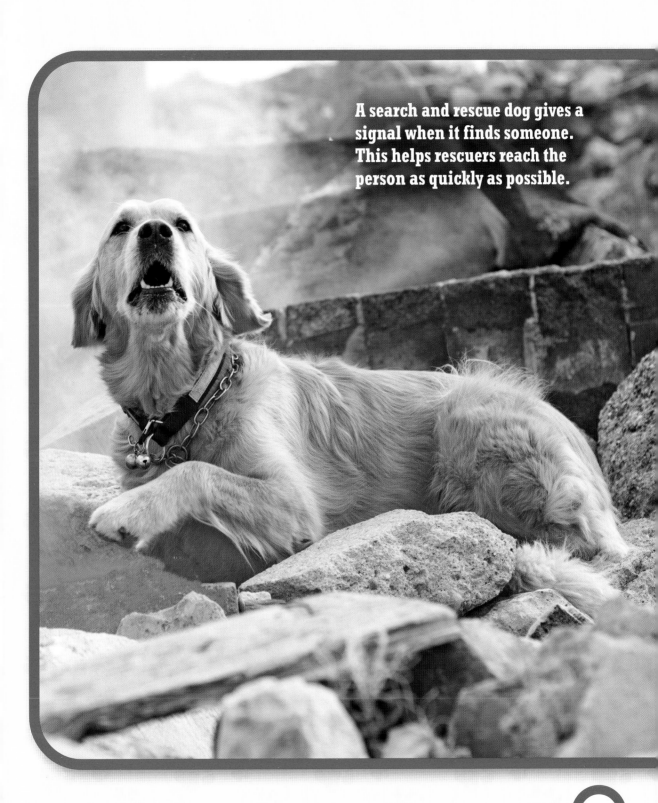

A search and rescue dog gives a signal when it finds someone. This helps rescuers reach the person as quickly as possible.

When Disaster Strikes

Search and rescue dogs are working dogs. They help find people who have become trapped or lost in mud or snow following **disasters** such as **mudslides** or **avalanches**. They look for people stuck inside broken buildings after earthquakes or tornadoes. These heroic dogs save hundreds of lives every year.

One dog can do the search work of 20 to 30 people! The dog's powerful sense of smell is the perfect tool for the job.

Search and rescue dogs also search for people who have gotten lost in nature.

What Does It Take?

Being a search and rescue dog is a hard job. As well as a great sense of smell, good search dogs need a lot of energy and **focus**. These dogs may need to work anywhere from four to eight hours at a time. They need to be strong, too. Search and rescue dogs often have to run, jump, and climb when they are working.

Bloodhounds have the best noses of all dogs. They can follow a scent for more than 130 miles (209 km). They can even find a scent that is 12 days old.

German shepherds often make good search and rescue dogs. They are strong and have thick fur that protects them in bad weather.

Working Like a Dog

It takes lots of training to become a search and rescue dog. Each promising pup works with a **handler** to get ready for the job. The dogs need to learn to stay focused, even among loud sounds or other distractions. They learn different ways to use their powerful noses to search for people. They also learn how to tell their handlers when they have found someone.

Search and rescue dogs have strong bonds with their handlers.

Many dogs begin their training as puppies. Search and rescue dog training can take up to 600 hours.

Super Noses

Once they are fully trained, search and rescue dogs are ready to work. If a person is lost, a handler and dog team will go the last place the person was seen. The handler will give the search dog something that belongs to the lost person, such as a shirt, so the dog knows what smell to search for. Then, the **canine** can follow the trail.

Dogs can smell 10,000 to 100,000 times better than humans. Talk about powerful sniffers!

When there's a lot of space that needs to be searched, more than one dog may be called in to help.

Another way search dogs work is to smell the air to find a scent. Air scenting can help find people trapped during disasters.

Better Together

After a search dog's super nose sniffs out a person in danger, it's time to tell the human half of the team. A search dog may **alert** its handler in many ways. Some dogs stay with the people they have found and bark to let their handlers know where they are. Others go back to their handlers and lead them to the people they've found.

Unlike many other working dogs, search and rescue dogs aren't always next to their handlers.

Often a search and rescue dog will work with only one handler. This makes the pair an even stronger team.

Fast on Four Legs

Besides their sense of smell, what else makes dogs so good at search and rescue work? Four fast legs! A dog can move quickly and easily across the uneven ground of the wilderness or over the rubble of a disaster zone. When people are in trouble, every second counts!

Search and rescue dogs often wear brightly colored vests, straps, or bandanas when they are working.

Search and rescue dogs are trained to make their way through disaster zones safely.

The Right Dog for the Job

Search and rescue dogs are usually trained for one type of search. Following a trail in the woods needs a different set of skills than searching through a broken building. Each dog gets a lot of **experience** in its area. And the more experience a dog has, the better it is at the job!

Some search and rescue dogs are trained to find other animals, such as lost pets.

Some search and rescue dogs work in water. They team up with divers who search underwater after the dogs give an alert.

19

Practice Makes Perfect

When there aren't people to help, how do search and rescue dogs keep their skills sharp? By practicing! Most search dogs practice every week. They practice in different places, day and night. Disasters can happen anywhere and at any time, so search and rescue dogs need to be ready.

Some search and rescue dogs learn to cross ladders. Others are trained to ride in helicopters.

When search and rescue dogs aren't working or training, they spend time with their families.

Meet a Real Search and Rescue Dog

Mason the golden retriever is an avalanche search and rescue dog at a ski resort in Colorado. He and his handler, Abby, have been a team since 2017. Mason loves to roll around in the snow, and resort visitors love to meet Mason! But it's not all fun and games. Every week, Mason and Abby practice their rescue skills on the slopes. They are ready to help when needed.

At the end of each day, Mason and Abby check the ski trails to make sure no one is hurt or needs help.

Glossary

alert to get a person's attention by touching, barking, or another action

avalanches large amounts of snow, ice, or dirt that move down mountains at fast speeds without warning

canines dogs

disasters events, such as earthquakes, that cause terrible destruction or harm

earthquake a sudden shaking of the ground caused by the moving of Earth's outer layer

experience skills or knowledge that you get by doing something

focus full attention given to something

handler a person who helps to train or manage a dog

mudslides large amounts of mud or dirt that move quickly down a hill

rescue to save from danger

rubble broken pieces of rock, brick, and other building materials

Index

Read More

Friesen, Helen Lepp. *Water Rescue Dogs (Dogs with Jobs)*. New York: AV2 by Weigl, 2020.

Laughlin, Kara L. *Search-And-Rescue Dogs (Dogs with Jobs)*. New York: AV2 by Weigl, 2019.

Learn More Online

1. Go to **www.factsurfer.com**
2. Enter "**Search and Rescue Dogs**" into the search box.
3. Click on the cover of this book to see a list of websites.

About the Author

Dale Jones lives in Los Angeles, California, with his family and two dogs.